FAULTS IN FIXATIONS

ADRITA CHATTERJI

Made with ♥ on the Notion Press Platform
www.notionpress.com

To everyone, I thought I'd never lose

but

lost.

Contents

Acknowledgements

If anyone I feel entitled to acknowledge as a must,
it is the gravity of time and its tides.

Introduction

When I started writing this book, I never knew I'd have to experience so much in order to legitimize the title of the same. Now that I've completed it, I hold it before the world to criticize. That isn't a symbol of validation for me though. Rather, if anything, the completion of the book is to aim for any lonely lost minds of its readers to not stop trying to paint their world with nothing other than their degree of absolute lunacy.

Trust me when I say this, Time is the supreme God and the wheel of it's dominion is itself a religion.

Have faith.

1. Hope

When I think of hope
I do not see black and white anymore
The colors smudge through a palette of vibrancy forming a rainbow
When I hear of hope
I do not listen to the murmurs of prayers outside a hospital
But the giggling of the young kids playing in the street
When I see hope
I'm not ashamed of the hypocrisy that the society showers with
Rather proud of humankind as it evolves, no matter how slow
When I smell hope
It doesn't remind me of the corpses and the carcasses post wars
But the petrichor after a season of scorching summer
When I taste hope
I'm not reminded of the charred cigarette I just turned into ashes
Rather the homemade ice cream Ma used to make on Sundays
Finally, when I get to touch hope
I'm not terrified of the first time I was held without consent
But the time I first felt how affection can be conveyed physically
You see, Hope is but the reason to hold on
Keeping faith in the commas
And not considering each passing season as a full stop
So next time, when it gets too hard
Just hold on - have faith in the passage of time;
For, this too shall pass

2. Conscience

When the night gets darker
And you know it's just the beginning
Remind yourself of your strength
And all the harder times that you've been in
For nothing but your conscience
Would stay when you sink in deep
Knowing the virtues that are now so valuable
But once you were unable to keep
Yet you kept going on
With each passing day
And the guilt consumed you alive
But you had no other option than to stay -
As you are
And as you've always been
Look around, human,
You're but being the redemption to each of your every single sin!
So keep holding on, please, would you?
Try to find the clause that pulls you aback
While creating history with everything that you are
But with everything more that apparently you lack

3. Sorry to Worry

When my ink grows shallow
And my thoughts linger over the last worry
I think of all the times when the night has passed
And all I felt, later, was sorry
For overanalyzing
Or provoking the remembrance of triggering traumas
Instead, I should have just slept
Not obsessing about the dramas
That kept repeating inside of my head
Making me feel as if I was being burnt alive
So hard to keep breathing
As each second was passing as a moment of strive
I wish I knew a little better
Or was a tad bit wiser
So many sleepless nights could have been saved
Followed by my passions of desire

4. Never Be Mine

Guess I don't want you to be another habit of mine
Guess I want you as you may come
And long for you in your absence
Guess I want to have you all to myself
But only through all the ways I can never have you
Completely by myself. To myself.
Guess I want to love you
Like I've loved none before.
Fate seems to play funny
For neither can I let you go nor can I make you stay
As if like a wild wind, you're to come
And when gone, I'll be counting the uncertainties
In hope of seeing you again.
As time would may.
I've loved you in so many ways, mademoiselle,
Like I've never loved one before.
With a tiny tinge of blueish heart, in me
That even finds peace if you never become mine.
Entirely or remotely.
To love you in a manner so selfless
Is a whole process of rediscovery within me
Of being capable to withhold an unfamiliar love language
Or the ways I've known to express love
Through my creations and destructions.

To love you is to unlearn so many stigmas
That within me I've bore for far too long
Turning everyone I've ever loved, leave.
So, I want to hold you too delicately
As if I want to lose you
In my thoughts, never,
If not in physicality
And long for you in your absence
Making all of you worthwhile in your presence
Meanwhile carrying all the thoughts,
That lingers, of you, in my mind, within me.

5. Impossible Love

Everytime I've loved someone
I felt a passion of solace
But to save them from their nightmares
I've often been burnt out in the process
And whilst chasing impossible love
Is a psychological indication of my childhood tragedies
Nothing have I wanted evermore
Than to stay drenched in lovesick melancholies

6. Calm in Chaos

You are but that calm storm
Which I longed to see
To live a life with you, though apart,
I'll become everything I should be
To stay ultimately calm in utmost chaos
Would pen the epitome of my rage
While my sadness will linger over the last remains
Of the ink that scribbled on a blank page
I'll write in sanity henceforth
My toxicity is enough of an intoxication
That which I thought makes me, me;
Was nothing but just another distraction
The details of my artistry would be breath taking
I don't want happiness that's short-living
For the instability grows inside the vessel evermore
When the water in it starts outpouring
I'll embrace my chaos going forth
For I've nothing left to loose
If my peace lies in the nomadicity
Staying calm in chaos is now what I choose

7. BnW

Standing outside
You won't get who in me resides
As I look at you,
You'd feel it is the same person, just yellow or blue
But neither am I of any of the colors
I savor white and black
An aggravated conscience led by a devil's hand of anarchy
I wonder if you ever get it.
If you ever get the war that inside of me I fight -
Day night. For you. Against me. White vs Black.

Black has more hue, it darkens what White lightens.
And once a place is blackened, it can never be whitened again.
You don't get it.
Nobody does.
Nobody understands me thoroughly.
The triggers are so delicate and shallow.
White believes I'm above this, but Black is a lowlife.
It likes to dig through dirt.
Make me the culprit of something I endeavor.
I'm callous;
My heart is a wax castle
And I burn the wax
To keep me warm.

I'm beyond standards and prejudices
Yet I'm tied by the same.
Black and White is a game of chess
And my life hangs between either of the ends.

8. Begin from the Start

My words ignite a pyre of desire
As I disintegrate what once I prayed for
My allegories are but symphonies
Of the tragedy that dwells in me emerging a war
Why but my tongue
Once is so soothing for sores
Becomes the same tongue, though
That rips another heart to remorse
What are these afflictions?
Why does the persona changes attire?
So much unlove so easily achieved
Never being able to quench the thirst of it evermore
And I break myself brick by brick
With a believe in my hollow heart
That someday this war in me would stop
And I'd get a chance to begin from the start

9. Some Winter Noon

Hazily I remember a vision
As if from the future,
I'd come back to the moment -
Winter noon drenched in sunlight
I'm sitting by the window reading a book
Dad is cooking in the kitchen
With a humming way too familiar to ignore;
Accompanied by the occasional acoustical
Of my unmelodious sister
As she is dabbing on the laptop
Acting along the anomaly of an algorithm
Registered so deep in the conscience
That she is not even able to forget it in sleep;
Across me is lying my mobile phone
In which the face of my dear is evident
She has joined in with the humming chorus
Through her virtual presence
And my home has become so warm
At that very moment. At that very noon.
The forecast would be my prophecy
If I believe in the vision I'd felt
But this time I wasn't happy to feel the warmth
Rather afraid to lose it again.

10. Revelations

Why but you do not believe
That I'm but a man before you as I stand
My demons dance in different beats
Than yours, typically arrogant
Why but you do not believe
That I'm but a device of time and trauma
Reaching out to you requires me to unlearn more
Then learn customs as I've grown up without a mother
Why but you do not believe
That I try more than I can take
Maybe that is the reason I fail every time
As I keep on counting revelations through mistakes

The Epilogue

"As I end this tale of telling,
I want all of you to know
An artist am I at its epitome
And art is what I'd never let go"

Printed by Libri Plureos GmbH in Hamburg,
Germany